PIANO • VOCAL • GUITAR

CHART HITS
OF 2021-2022

ISBN 978-1-70516-099-2

Visit Hal Leonard Online at
www.halleonard.com

Contact us:
Hal Leonard
7777 West Bluemound Road
Milwaukee, WI 53213
Email: info@halleonard.com

In Europe, contact:
Hal Leonard Europe Limited
42 Wigmore Street
Marylebone, London, W1U 2RN
Email: info@halleonardeurope.com

In Australia, contact:
Hal Leonard Australia Pty. Ltd.
4 Lentara Court
Cheltenham, Victoria, 3192 Australia
Email: info@halleonard.com.au

ALL TOO WELL

Words and Music by TAYLOR SWIFT
and LIZ ROSE

EASY ON ME

Words and Music by ADELE ADKINS
and GREG KURSTIN

COLD HEART
(PNAU Remix)

Words and Music by ELTON JOHN,
BERNARD J.P. TAUPIN, NICHOLAS LITTLEMORE,
PETER MAYES, SAM LITTLEMORE,
DEAN MEREDITH and ANDREW JOHN MEECHAM

Recorded a half step lower.

FANCY LIKE

Words and Music by WALKER HAYES,
JOSH JENKINS, SHANE STEVENS
and CAMERON BARTOLINI

Moderately slow, in 2

* Recorded a half step lower. (Guitar is tuned down a half step.)

HEAT WAVES

Words and Music by
DAVE BAYLEY

Road shim-mer, wig-gl-ing the vi - sion. Heat, heat waves, _ I'm swim-ming in a mir-ror.

Road shim-mer, wig-gl-ing the vi - sion. Heat, heat waves, _ I'm swim-ming in a...

Recorded a half step lower.

Dm **C** **Am** **G**

Some - times all I think a - bout is you, _____ late _ nights in the mid - dle of June. _____

F **C** **Am/D** **G**

_____ Heat _ waves been fak - ing me _ out, _____ can't _ make you hap - pi - er _____ now. _____

Dm **C** **Am** **G**

U - sual - ly I put _ some - thing on T - V _____ so we nev - er think _ a - bout you and me. _

F **C** **Am/D** **G**

_____ But to - day I see _ our re - flec - tions clear - ly in Hol - ly - wood _ lay - ing on the screen. _

FOLLOW YOU

Words and Music by DAN REYNOLDS,
WAYNE SERMON, BEN McKEE,
DANIEL PLATZMAN, ELLEY DUHÉ,
JOEL LITTLE and FRANSISCA HALL

GHOST

Words and Music by JUSTIN BIEBER,
JONATHAN BELLION, JORDAN JOHNSON,
STEFAN JOHNSON and MICHAEL POLLACK

Young blood thinks there's al - ways to - mor - row.
Young blood thinks there's al - ways to - mor - row.

I miss your touch on nights ___ when I'm hol - low.
Need more time, but time ___ can't be bor - rowed.

I miss you more than ___ life. more than ___ life.

So if I

can't get close ___ to you I'll set - tle for the

MY UNIVERSE

Words and Music by CHRIS MARTIN,
WILL CHAMPION, JON BUCKLAND,
GUY BERRYMAN, MAX MARTIN,
HO-SEOK JUNG, NAM-JOON KIM,
YOON-GI MIN, OSCAR HOLTER
and BILL RAHKO

Moderate Pop

You, you are my u - ni - verse_ and __ I just want to

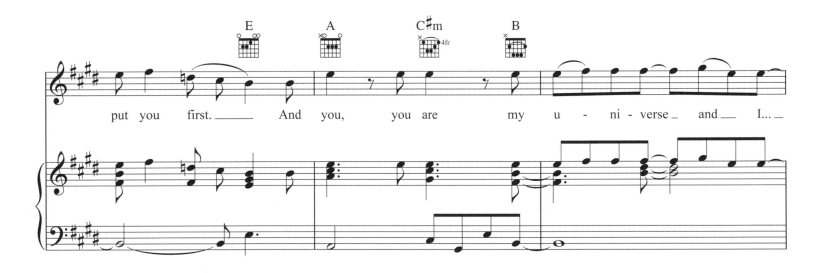

put you first.___ And you, you are my u - ni - verse_ and __ I....__

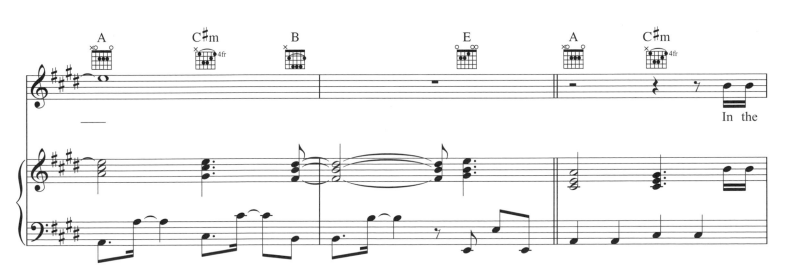

In the

* Romanization of Korean lyrics.

HAPPIER THAN EVER

Words and Music by BILLIE EILISH O'CONNELL
and FINNEAS O'CONNELL

When I'm a-way from

you, I'm hap-pi-er than ev - er. Wish I could ex-plain it bet -

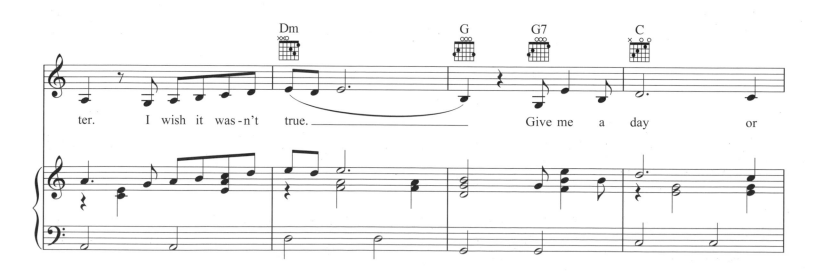

ter. I wish it was-n't true. _____ Give me a day or

two to think of some-thing ___ clev - er, to write my-self a let -

ter to tell me what to do. ___

Do you read my in - ter-views or ___ do you skip my

av - e - nue? When you said you were pass - in' through, was I ___

IF I DIDN'T LOVE YOU

Words and Music by KURT ALLISON,
TULLY KENNEDY, JOHN MORGAN
and LYDIA VAUGHAN

Moderately

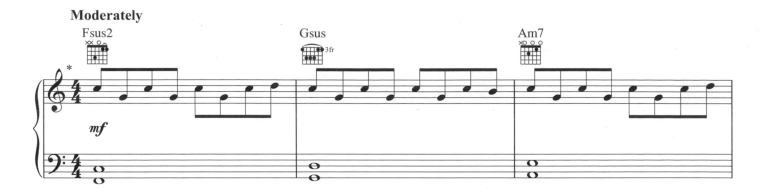

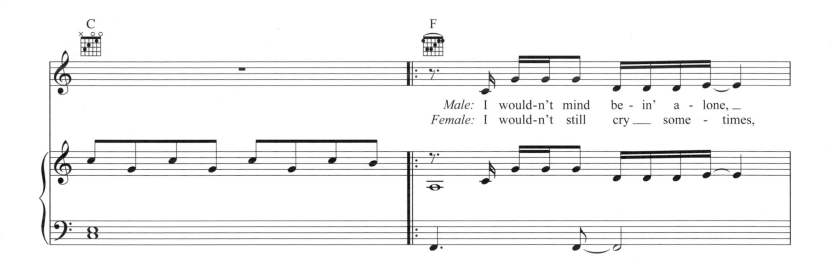

Male: I would-n't mind be-in' a - lone, __
Female: I would-n't still cry __ some - times,

I would-n't keep check-in' my phone, __ would-n't take the long __ way home __ just to
would-n't have to fake a smile, __ play it off and tell __ a lie __ when __

* Recorded a half step higher.

IT'LL BE OKAY

Words and Music by SHAWN MENDES,
SCOTT HARRIS, MICHAEL SABATH,
and EDDIE BENJAMIN

Moderately slow

Are we gon - na make ___ it? Is this gon - na hurt?

Oh, we can try to se - date ___ it, but that nev - er works,

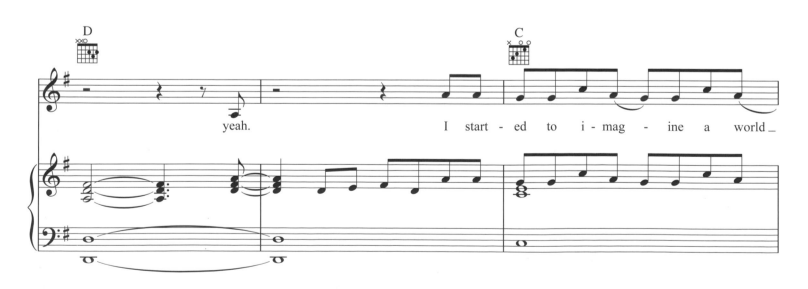

yeah. I start - ed to i - mag - ine a world ___

LOVE AGAIN

Words and Music by DUA LIPA,
CLARENCE BERNARD COFFEE, CHELCEE GRIMES,
STEPHEN KOZMENIUK, BING CROSBY,
IRVING WALLMAN and MAX WARTELL

Moderately fast

I nev-er thought that I would find a way out. __
I used to think that I was made out of stone. __
So man-y nights my tears fell hard-er than rain, __

I nev-er thought I'd hear my heart beat so loud. __
I used to spend so man-y nights on my own. __
scared I would take my bro-ken heart to the grave. __

I can't be-lieve there's some-thing
I nev-er knew I had it
I'd rath-er die than have to

* Vocal written one octave higher than sung.

SHIVERS

Words and Music by ED SHEERAN,
JOHNNY McDAID, STEVE MAC
and KAL LAVELLE

PERMISSION TO DANCE

Words and Music by ED SHEERAN,
JOHNNY McDAID, STEVE MAC
and JENNA ANDREWS

STAY

Words and Music by JUSTIN BIEBER,
BLAKE SLATKIN, OMER FEDI,
CHARLIE PUTH, CHARLTON HOWARD,
MAGNUS HOLBERG, MICHAEL MULE,
ISSAC DeBONI and SUBHAAN RAHMAN

Moderate Synth Pop

I do the same ___ thing I told you that I nev-er would. I

told you I changed, e-ven when I knew I nev-er could. I

* Recorded a half step lower.

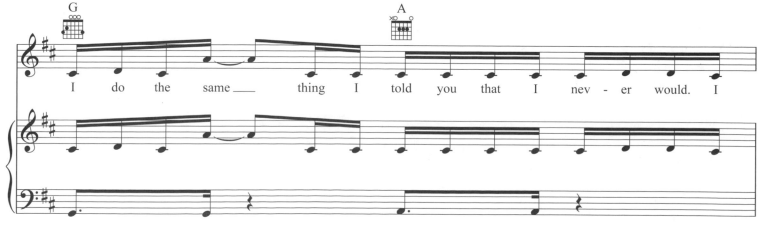

TAKE MY BREATH

Words and Music by ABEL TESFAYE,
MAX MARTIN, OSCAR HOLTER
and AHMAD BALSHE

Dance Pop

I saw the fi - re in your eyes. _____

I saw the fi - re when I looked _ in - to your eyes.

You tell me things _ you want to try. _____

WE DON'T TALK ABOUT BRUNO

from ENCANTO

Music and Lyrics by
LIN-MANUEL MIRANDA

DOLORES:

We don't talk a - bout Bru - no! _____ Hey!

We don't talk a - bout Bru - no! _____

Grew to live in fear of Bru - no stut - ter - ing or stumb - ling, I can al - ways hear him sort of mut - ter - ing and mum - bling.

I as - so - ci - ate him with the sound of fall - ing sand, ch ch ch

* Vocal sung an octave lower than written.

PEPA, FÉLIX
CAMILO & DOLORES:

We don't talk a-bout Bru - no, no, ___ no, ___ no!
We don't talk a - bout Bru - no, ___ no! ___

We don't talk a - bout Bru - no! ___
We don't talk a - bout Bru - no!

TOWNSWOMAN
WITH FISH:

TOWNSPEOPLE:

He told me my fish would die. ___ The next ___ day: dead. No, ___ no!

OSVALDO:

SEÑOR FLORES:

He told me I'd grow a gut! And just like he said... He said that

TOWNSPEOPLE: (No, ___ no!)

Cm   Ab

-er would grow, ___ like the grapes   that   thrive ___ on the vine... ___

Eb   Bb

ABUELA ALMA:

___ Ó - ye, Ma - ria - no's on his way

DOLORES: He   told   me   that   the   man

Cm   Ab

of my dreams would be just   out of reach,   be - trothed to an - oth - er...

Eb   Bb

It's like I hear him ___ now. ___

ISABELA:

Hey sis, ___   I   want

* Vocal sung an octave lower than written.

* *Vocal sung at pitch.*

SMOKIN' OUT THE WINDOW

Words and Music by PETER GENE HERNANDEZ,
DERNST EMILE and ANDERSON .PAAK

Freely

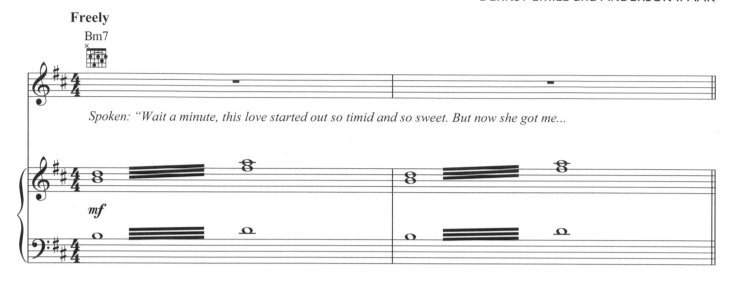

Spoken: "Wait a minute, this love started out so timid and so sweet. But now she got me...

mf

In time, moderate groove

Smok- in' out the win - dow. _____

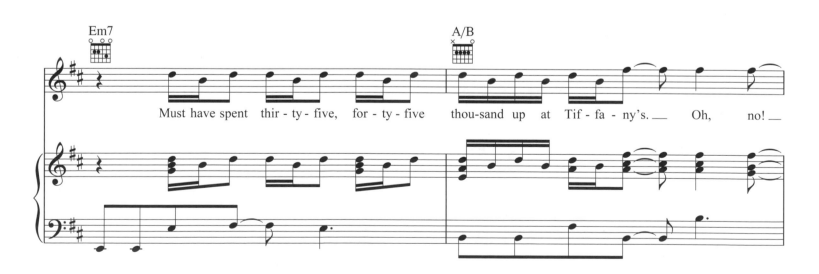

Must have spent thir-ty-five, for-ty-five thou-sand up at Tif-fa-ny's. _____ Oh, no! _____

Ba - by, why you do - ing this? Why you do - ing this___ to me,_____ girl?

Not to be dra - ma - tic, but I want___ to die._____ This bitch got me

- 'ry - bod - y, ooh. ____

Spoken: "Look here baby, I hope you found whatever it is that you need. But I also hope that your trifling ass is walking 'round